Donald Trump?

A Teen's Guide to the Life and Journey of a Prominent Figure

Steven Clowers

Copyright

Copyright ©Steven Clowers2023

All rights reserved. No part of this publication may be reproduced, distributed, or transmitted in any form or by any means, including photocopying, recording, or other electronic or mechanical methods, without the prior written permission of the publisher, except in the case of brief quotations embodied in critical reviews and certain other noncommercial uses permitted by copyright law.

This book is a work of non-fiction and is based on the research and experiences of the author. While every effort has been made to ensure the accuracy and completeness of the information presented, the author and the publisher assume no responsibility for errors or omissions, or for damages resulting from the use of the information contained herein.

Who is this book for?

Teens:

This book is tailor-made for curious and forward-thinking teens who are eager to explore the lives of prominent figures and the intricate stories that have shaped their paths. If you're a teen with a hunger for knowledge, an interest in history, or a curiosity about the people who have left their mark on the world, "Daddy, Who is Donald Trump?" is here to satisfy your quest for understanding. Whether you're drawn to his accomplishments, captivated by his journey, or intrigued by the lessons he learned, this book provides an engaging narrative that resonates with your aspirations and fuels your desire to learn from the lives of those who came before.

Parents:

For parents, this book offers an opportunity to bridge generations and engage in meaningful conversations with your children. As role models and guides, parents play a pivotal role in shaping their children's understanding of the world. "Daddy, Who is Donald Trump?" serves as a springboard for discussing topics like resilience, family values, determination, and the complex path to success. Through the lens of Donald Trump's life, you can explore these themes together, helping your children cultivate critical thinking skills, empathy, and an appreciation for the diverse tapestry of human experience. Whether you're reading alongside your teens or sparking discussions about the lessons drawn from Trump's journey, this book serves as a valuable resource for nurturing conversations that transcend generations.

Why do you need to learn about Donald Trump?

Understanding Donald Trump's journey offers valuable insights:

- Learn resilience from his challenges.
- Explore diverse viewpoints and perspectives.
- Apply ambition, discipline, and leadership to your growth.
- Understand the influence of family values.
- Gain historical awareness and global impact insights.
- Enhance conversations on politics and contemporary issues.
- Draw inspiration for setting and achieving goals.

- Develop critical thinking and open-mindedness.
- Apply lessons learned to your own life journey.

CONTENT

Who is this book for?...................... 3
Why do you need to learn about Donald Trump?.................................6
Introduction..................................... 10
Chapter 1... 14
   Who is Donald Trump?............... 14
Chapter 2... 17
Teenage Life and Education........ 17
Chapter 3... 23
His School Days............................23
   Kew-Forest School..................... 23
   New York Military Academy (NYMA)...28
   Fordham University in New York 33
   Wharton School of Business at the University of Pennsylvania.......... 37
Chapter 4... 40
The Real Estate Magnet................40

Influence of Father's Business....44
Chapter 5... 56
You are fired!.................................56
Chapter 6... 63
Stepping into the World of Politics............ 63
Chapter 7... 74
Lessons from Donald Trump....... 74
The Conclusion............................79

Introduction

In the tapestry of history, certain figures emerge as captivating enigmas, leaving an indelible mark on the world's canvas. One such figure is Donald Trump, a name that has echoed through the spheres of business, entertainment, and politics. But the question remains: "Who is Donald Trump?" What threads weave together to create the tapestry of his life and journey?

Welcome to "Daddy, Who is Donald Trump?" This book is an invitation to embark on a captivating voyage, a journey that navigates the intricacies of a prominent personality whose story spans generations. In these pages, you'll unearth the captivating chapters of a multifaceted individual's life, exploring not only the headlines but the heartbeats behind them.

From his youth in Queens, New York, to the rise of an iconic real estate titan and the allure of television fame, to a seat at the helm of the nation as the 45th President of the United States—Donald Trump's story unfolds with intrigue and insight. Here, you'll discover the life lessons drawn from family, the crucibles that stoked his ambitions, and the unyielding resilience that propelled him through trials and triumphs.

In this journey, we invite you to witness defining moments: choices that altered destinies, audacious endeavors that left their mark, and the tenacious faith that stood strong in the face of challenge. This is more than just a recollection of events—it's a guided exploration into the tapestry of attributes that form a fascinating figure. Traits like leadership, resilience, and the ability to craft dreams into reality become not just words on a page but inspirations for aspiring hearts.

With a keen eye and open heart, delve into "Daddy, Who is Donald Trump?" as we unravel not only the enigma but the enduring lessons that emerge from his journey. A journey that, at its core, resonates with the aspirations of those seeking direction and guidance, offering insights into the power of determination, the influence of family bonds, and the resolute spirit that propels individuals to paint their own legacies on the canvas of time.

Chapter 1

Who is Donald Trump?

His Background

Donald Trump was born on June 14, 1946, in Queens, New York City. He grew up in a well-to-do family, with his father, Fred Trump, being a successful real estate developer. Trump's exposure to his father's business ventures and properties from an early age likely played a role in shaping his interest in real estate.

He attended the Kew-Forest School in Queens and later the New York Military Academy (NYMA) in upstate New York during his teenage years. At NYMA, he developed leadership skills and discipline that would influence his later life.

After graduating from NYMA, Trump attended Fordham University for two years before transferring to the Wharton School of Finance at the University of Pennsylvania, where he earned a degree in economics.

His early experiences within a family of real estate developers, coupled with his education, laid the groundwork for his future ventures in the real estate industry. Trump's background in real estate and his exposure to business practices within his family undoubtedly played a significant role in shaping his career trajectory and eventual prominence in business, entertainment, and politics.

His Early life

Donald John Trump grew up in Queens, New York City. He was the fourth of five children in his family. His father was a successful real estate developer, and his mother was a homemaker from Scotland. Trump attended a private school in Queens and later went to the New York Military Academy. He excelled in sports and leadership roles during his time there. Afterward, he attended the University of Pennsylvania's Wharton School of Finance, where he earned a degree in economics. These early experiences and influences played a significant role in shaping his future endeavors.

Chapter 2

Teenage Life and Education

Adolescence and Personal Development

As the pages of Donald Trump's life turned from childhood to adolescence, a transformational period of personal development unfolded. This phase marked the beginning of his journey to becoming a figure of prominence, shaping the values, skills, and outlook that would guide his future endeavors.

Sports and Athletics

Amid the myriad challenges and opportunities of adolescence, sports emerged as a defining outlet for Donald Trump. He didn't merely participate; he immersed himself wholeheartedly. From football to baseball and soccer, his engagement in sports was not just about competition—it was about embracing discipline, teamwork, and the pursuit of excellence.

In the realm of sports, Trump discovered more than just physical prowess; he discovered the power of dedication and the ability to thrive within a team. These attributes would later become pillars of his leadership philosophy, influencing his business acumen and his approach to challenges.

Educational Path: Fordham University and Wharton School

While the allure of sports captivated his teenage years, the intellectual realm was equally compelling. The tapestry of his teenage life wove through academic corridors that shaped his understanding of business, economics, and leadership.

His academic journey began at Fordham University, where he embarked on a course that would lay the groundwork for his future achievements. Within the hallowed halls of this institution, he encountered the world of finance, economics, and intellectual exploration—each contributing a thread to the fabric of his burgeoning ambitions.

Yet, it was at the Wharton School of Finance at the University of Pennsylvania that the tapestry of his destiny truly unfolded. Here, surrounded by an environment of intellectual fervor and innovation, Trump's educational odyssey transformed into a crucible of ambition and insight.

The Wharton School became the incubator for his aspirations. Amidst classrooms buzzing with ideas and corridors resonating with academic fervor, he honed his financial acumen and cultivated his entrepreneurial spirit. It was a place where theories met practice, where concepts were forged into strategies, and where intellectual engagement melded with visionary thinking.

Within the crucible of academia, Donald Trump's passion for business and economics took root, propelling him toward the precipice of his future success. The lessons learned within these walls would serve as the bedrock of his endeavors in real estate, entrepreneurship, and public life.

As he transitioned from adolescence to adulthood, the confluence of personal growth, sportsmanship, and academic pursuit set the stage for the emergence of a dynamic individual—one who would go on to reshape industries, challenge norms, and leave an indelible mark on the world stage. The teenage years of Donald Trump became the tapestry of his ascent—a journey that would eventually capture the world's attention and inspire the generations that followed.

Chapter 3

His School Days

Kew-Forest School

When Donald Trump was a young boy, he attended the Kew-Forest School, a private school located in Queens, New York City. He started his education there in kindergarten and continued through the seventh grade.

During his time at Kew-Forest, Trump was known for his energetic and lively personality. He was an active student who enjoyed participating in various activities. He was part of the school's baseball team and even sported a baseball cap with his name on it.

One memorable story from his Kew-Forest days is when he was in second grade. It's said that he once stood up to his music teacher, suggesting that the teacher didn't know enough about music. This incident might seem surprising, but it reflects Trump's strong opinions and confidence, even at a young age.

He was also recognized for his love of sports and competition, traits that stayed with him throughout his life. Although he eventually moved on from Kew-Forest, his time there likely influenced his early personality and interests significantly.

During his years at Kew-Forest, Trump wasn't just known for his lively personality and involvement in sports; he also had a knack for standing out in various ways:

1. Confidence in Debates: Even as a young student, Trump was known for being outspoken and confident. He would engage in debates with his classmates and wasn't afraid to voice his opinions on different topics.

2. Leadership in Class: Trump often took the lead in group projects and classroom discussions. He displayed leadership qualities that would later become a significant part of his public image.

3.Business Ventures: Trump's entrepreneurial spirit started early. He once sold lemonade to his classmates during hot days, showing his interest in business and making a little money on the side.

4. Sense of Style: Trump was known for his sense of fashion even back then. He had a distinctive hairstyle and was particular about his appearance, setting him apart from his peers.

5. Popularity: Trump was well-liked by many of his classmates. His energetic and enthusiastic nature made him stand out and drew people to him.

6. Love for Learning: While he had a strong personality, he was also curious and eager to learn. He had an interest in various subjects, including history and economics.

7. Influence of Teachers: Some of Trump's teachers at Kew-Forest noticed his potential and encouraged him to pursue his interests. This support likely contributed to his drive to succeed.

8. Interactions with Peers: Trump had a wide circle of friends and interacted with students from diverse backgrounds. This exposure might have contributed to his ability to connect with people from different walks of life later in his career.

These events highlight different aspects of Trump's character during his time at Kew-Forest. From debates and leadership to his business mindset and interactions with peers, his experiences there helped shape the foundation of the person he would become.

So, Trump's time at the Kew-Forest School was characterized by his spirited nature, active participation in sports, and his willingness to express his thoughts. Little did anyone know that this young student would eventually become a major figure in business and politics!

New York Military Academy (NYMA).

When Donald Trump was a teenager, he attended the New York Military Academy (NYMA), a boarding school located in Cornwall-on-Hudson, New York. He enrolled at NYMA in 1959 and stayed there until he graduated in 1964. This period had a significant impact on shaping his personality, values, and approach to life.

At NYMA, Trump's days were structured and disciplined. The academy had a military-style environment, with students wearing uniforms and adhering to a strict schedule. This routine was designed to instill discipline, responsibility, and time-management skills in the students.

One of the key aspects of NYMA was its emphasis on leadership development. Trump was exposed to leadership opportunities through various roles and responsibilities. He held positions such as cadet captain and student leader, which allowed him to practice decision-making and delegation early on.

Similar to his time at Kew-Forest, Trump continued to engage in sports at NYMA. He played football, baseball, and basketball, demonstrating his commitment to physical fitness and teamwork. Competing in sports contributed to his sense of camaraderie and determination.

NYMA also prioritized academics. The academy aimed to prepare students for college and beyond. Trump's time at NYMA allowed him to develop his academic skills and critical thinking abilities, which he would later apply to his business ventures.

The strict rules and regulations at NYMA taught Trump the importance of following rules, taking responsibility for his actions, and being accountable for his choices. These values would become integral to his leadership style in the business world.

During his time at NYMA, Trump built relationships with peers, teachers, and mentors. These connections provided him with a network of individuals who would play a role in his future endeavors.

NYMA encouraged students to develop their public speaking skills. Trump participated in debates and public speaking competitions, honing his ability to articulate his thoughts and project confidence – skills he would later use during his campaigns and speeches.

The military structure of NYMA had a lasting influence on Trump. He often spoke about how the academy's discipline, organization, and emphasis on hierarchy shaped his approach to managing his businesses and making decisions.

Ultimately, NYMA provided Trump with a well-rounded education that extended beyond academics. It instilled in him values of discipline, leadership, and determination that contributed to his future successes in real estate, entertainment, and politics.

Graduating from NYMA marked a transition for Trump from adolescence to adulthood. The experiences, values, and skills he gained during his time there laid the foundation for his future ventures and played a pivotal role in his journey to becoming a prominent figure in American public life.

Fordham University in New York

After finishing military school, Trump went on to study at Fordham University in New York for a couple of years before transferring to the Wharton School at the University of Pennsylvania.

Picture this: back in the swinging sixties, a young and ambitious Donald Trump was making his mark at Fordham University in the heart of New York City. Fresh out of the New York Military Academy, he was ready to take on the world!

With his eyes set on the business world, Trump dove headfirst into the world of academia, focusing on all things business. He joined the cool Phi Gamma Delta (FIJI) fraternity, rubbing shoulders with future movers and shakers. Think of it as a real-life "frat house" adventure.

But that's not all. Did you know that before conquering the real estate scene, Trump had dreams of becoming a Hollywood big shot? Yep, he dreamed of producing movies! It's like he had a secret plan to take over the entertainment world before he even tackled the business empire.

Then, in a move that changed his path forever, Trump decided to make a big leap.

He hopped over to the prestigious Wharton School of Business at the University of Pennsylvania. Imagine the excitement of packing his bags and setting off to conquer new horizons.

Now, while we might not have all the juicy details of his Fordham days, we can imagine him juggling books, parties, and maybe even some wild adventures around the streets of New York. Who knows what kind of cool stories and unforgettable memories he made during those years?

So, the next time you walk past Fordham University or hear about Donald Trump's journey, remember that even the most powerful figures had their own awesome teenage years full of dreams, surprises, and exciting twists!

During his school days, Trump learned a lot about negotiation and business deals from his father, who was a successful real estate developer. These lessons stuck with him and played a big role in his later business ventures.

So, Donald Trump's school days were a mix of military discipline, sports, and learning about economics. His experiences in school, along with the values he learned, would shape his journey from a teenager to a major player in the business and political world.

Wharton School of Business at the University of Pennsylvania.

Buckle up, because the tale of Donald Trump's time at the Wharton School of Business is quite the rollercoaster ride! In 1966, he traded in the Bronx for the city of brotherly love, where he embarked on a journey that would shape his destiny.

Imagine a young Trump, armed with ambition and a thirst for success, striding through the ivy-covered halls of Wharton. With his eyes set on the world of business, he dove headfirst into his studies, eager to learn the ropes of the trade.

But hold on tight, because here comes the exciting part: his larger-than-life personality wasn't confined to the classroom. Trump's charisma and knack for networking came alive at Wharton. He wasn't just another student; he was a force to be reckoned with. Those connections he made? They'd become the building blocks of his empire.

Heated debates in the lecture halls, intense discussions about economics and finance, and Trump's undeniable presence at the center of it all. He wasn't just there to learn; he was there to conquer.

And conquer he did. In 1968, with a Bachelor of Science in Economics in hand, Trump graduated from Wharton, ready to take on the world of business. Little did he know that his time at Wharton was just the beginning of a saga that would see him rise to become a household name.

So, whether he was mastering the art of the deal in class or forging connections that would shape his future, Trump's days at the Wharton School of Business were a pivotal chapter in his journey to becoming the icon we know today.

Chapter 4

The Real Estate Magnet

Donald Trump, the 45th President of the United States, is renowned for his background as a real estate tycoon before venturing into politics. He inherited his passion for real estate from his father, Fred Trump, a successful real estate developer. Before his political career, Donald Trump made a name for himself as a charismatic and ambitious developer.

One of his early significant projects was the transformation of the Commodore Hotel in Manhattan, rebranding it as the Grand Hyatt

New York in 1980. This marked his entry into the world of high-profile real estate developments. However, Trump's most notable achievements are his series of skyscrapers, with Trump Tower on Fifth Avenue in New York City being the pinnacle. Completed in 1983, Trump Tower showcases his penchant for lavish design and effective marketing.

Guided by his leadership, the Trump Organization, established by his paternal grandmother Elizabeth Christ Trump and expanded by his father, played a crucial role in building his real estate empire. Under his guidance, the organization acquired and developed properties across various sectors, including residential, commercial, hospitality, and entertainment. Trump's real estate ventures extended beyond New York City, encompassing properties in major cities and countries.

Another milestone in his real estate journey was the completion of the Trump Taj Mahal casino in Atlantic City in 1990. Despite its initial success, financial challenges led the project to declare bankruptcy. This event marked one of several instances where Trump's businesses faced financial difficulties. Nevertheless, Trump remained a significant player in the real estate industry, using his brand and media presence to draw attention to his projects.

During the early 2000s, Trump entered reality television with shows like "The Apprentice," further enhancing his public image and brand recognition. His persona as a savvy businessman and dealmaker became deeply ingrained in the public consciousness. Throughout his career, Trump's real estate approach was defined by calculated risks, high-profile negotiations, and a combination of grandeur and controversy in promoting his developments.

It's important to acknowledge that Trump's real estate career wasn't devoid of controversy. He encountered legal disputes, bankruptcy filings, and criticisms regarding his business practices and ethics. Despite these challenges, his legacy as a real estate mogul is undeniable, as he left an enduring impact on the industry through ambitious projects, innovative marketing, and an ability to generate headlines.

In 2016, Trump transitioned from real estate to politics, winning the U.S. presidential election and assuming office in January 2017. While his political career marked a departure from his previous endeavors, his influence on the real estate world remains an integral part of his legacy.

Influence of Father's Business

Donald Trump's trajectory as a real estate magnate was significantly influenced by his father's business ventures. His father, Fred Trump, was a prominent figure in the New York real estate scene, having developed residential properties in Brooklyn and Queens. Growing up in this environment exposed Donald Trump to the intricacies of real estate from a young age. He often accompanied his father to construction sites and absorbed valuable insights into the industry's operations.

Fred Trump's company, Elizabeth Trump & Son, played a pivotal role in Donald Trump's early career. The company's projects ranged from middle-class housing to luxury apartment complexes, providing him with a comprehensive understanding of various market segments. These experiences laid the foundation for his later ventures and shaped his approach to business.

When Donald Trump joined the Trump Organization in the 1960s, he brought his father's business lessons with him. Working alongside his father, he learned the art of dealmaking, negotiation, and property management. He also developed a keen eye for identifying promising real estate opportunities, a skill that would prove instrumental in his future endeavors.

The Trump Organization's expansion into Manhattan marked a turning point for both Donald and the company. With Fred Trump's guidance and resources, they ventured into more high-profile projects. Donald's vision for upscale, luxury properties aligned with the company's newfound direction, allowing him to carve out his niche in the competitive New York real estate landscape.

Inheriting the business acumen of his father, Donald Trump further refined his skills by navigating the challenges of real estate development. He adapted to market trends, implemented innovative marketing strategies, and showcased an unwavering determination to succeed. While he encountered setbacks along the way, his father's influence remained a constant source of inspiration and guidance.

As Donald Trump's real estate empire grew, he carried forward his father's legacy while also forging his own path. The lessons learned from Fred Trump's business endeavors continued to inform his decision-making and shaped his unique style of leadership within the Trump Organization.

In essence, Fred Trump's successful foray into real estate and his mentorship of Donald Trump laid the groundwork for the latter's ascent to becoming a real estate magnate. The family legacy, coupled with Donald Trump's innate business instincts and unwavering drive, propelled him to leave an indelible mark on the real estate industry that extended far beyond his father's achievements.

For today's teens, delving into the story of Donald Trump's rise as a real estate magnate offers not only a glimpse into the world of business and entrepreneurship but also a lesson in the power of determination and innovation. Imagine being a teenager with a passion for big dreams and ambitions –

Donald Trump's journey can serve as a source of inspiration and insight.

Think about it: just like you, Trump started with an idea and a drive to make it big. From his early exposure to his father's real estate projects to his eventual ownership of skyscrapers and luxury properties, he demonstrated how a strong foundation of knowledge and an unwavering commitment to his goals can lead to extraordinary achievements.

As a teenager, you might be curious about how the real estate industry works and what it takes to turn a vision into reality. Trump's story can offer valuable lessons about risk-taking, strategic planning, and creative problem-solving. He learned to navigate challenges, adapt to changing market conditions, and market his properties effectively – skills that are applicable in various fields, not just real estate.

Additionally, Trump's transition into reality television with shows like "The Apprentice" highlights the importance of building a personal brand and using media to your advantage. In today's digital age, understanding the power of branding and effective communication is crucial for anyone looking to stand out and make an impact.

While Trump's journey was not without controversy, his experiences also underline the importance of ethics, integrity, and responsible decision-making in business. As a teenager, learning from both successes and failures can help shape your own path and set you up for success in the long run.

Whether you're considering a future in real estate, business, or any other field, Donald Trump's story can serve as a roadmap for achieving your dreams. His transformation from a young enthusiast to a real estate magnate and beyond shows that with the right mindset, dedication, and a willingness to learn, you have the potential to shape your own success story.

There are some more cool things that happened in Donald Trump's real estate career that you might find interesting:

1. Chicago's Tower of Luxury: Imagine a super tall building with fancy hotel rooms, cool condos, and shops. That's what Donald Trump made happen with the Trump International Hotel and Tower in Chicago. It was finished in 2009 and showed how he could make buildings look awesome in different cities.

2. Super Fancy Mar-a-Lago: Ever heard of a place that was once a fancy house and then turned into a private club? Well, that's Mar-a-Lago in Florida. Donald Trump got it in 1985 and turned it into a super fancy club and resort. It's all about luxury and being super exclusive.

3. Golf and Resorts Everywhere: Did you know Trump was into golf courses and fancy resorts too? He got some super cool places like Trump National Doral in Miami and Trump Turnberry in Scotland. These places show how he wanted to bring luxury and class to different parts of the world.

4.Using His Name Everywhere: Imagine if other people could use your name to make their stuff cooler. Well, that's what Trump did with real estate. He let others use his name for their buildings to make them look more high-class. But sometimes this led to problems and arguments.

5. Historic Building Turned Hotel: Ever been to Washington, D.C.? There's this cool building called the Old Post Office Pavilion. Trump transformed it into a fancy hotel in 2016. This project was all about making history look modern and cool at the same time.

6. Books and Learning: Trump wrote some books that give you tips about business, real estate, and being a great dealmaker. His books like "The Art of the Deal" and "Think Big and Kick Ass" share his ideas on how to make things happen.

7. Ups and Downs: Even though he had a lot of success, Trump also faced some tough times, like when some of his projects didn't do well and he had money problems. These tough times show that even successful people have challenges to deal with.

So, there you have it! Donald Trump's real estate journey is like an adventure filled with fancy buildings, cool ideas, and some challenges along the way. It's a reminder that with big dreams and hard work, you can make really amazing things happen in the world of real estate and beyond.

Chapter 5

You are fired!

Donald Trump's journey to fame took an intriguing turn with his role on the reality TV show "The Apprentice." This marked a significant transition from his previous ventures in real estate and business. The catchphrase "You're Fired!" became synonymous with his persona on the show, propelling him into the spotlight and solidifying his place in pop culture. The show's popularity played a pivotal role in shaping the public's perception of Trump, setting the stage for his future endeavors in politics and beyond.

As the host of "The Apprentice," Donald Trump showcased his business acumen and leadership style to a wide audience. His straightforward and often blunt approach, epitomized by the phrase "You're Fired!", resonated with viewers and contributed to the show's success. The catchphrase not only became a cultural reference but also emphasized Trump's decisive and no-nonsense demeanor.

The show's format, which revolved around contestants competing in various business-related challenges, allowed Trump to display his expertise in deal-making and decision-making. His role as the ultimate authority figure added an element of drama, keeping viewers engaged as they anticipated who would be eliminated next. This combination of business insights and entertainment value contributed to the show's popularity and Trump's growing celebrity status.

"The Apprentice" served as a platform for Trump to reinforce his brand as a successful entrepreneur and a tough, results-oriented leader. The exposure he gained from the show expanded his reach beyond the business world, making him a recognizable figure in households across the nation. This newfound visibility would eventually play a role in his decision to enter the political arena, a move that would change the course of his career and American politics as a whole.

The success of "The Apprentice" not only bolstered Donald Trump's public image but also provided him with a unique platform to connect with a diverse audience. The show's popularity allowed him to reach beyond his real estate endeavors and connect with people from various walks of life. This increased visibility paved the way for his transition from the world of television to the realm of politics.

The catchphrase "You're Fired!" became emblematic of Trump's leadership style, portraying him as someone unafraid to make tough decisions and hold individuals accountable. This portrayal resonated with a segment of the population that admired his assertiveness and business acumen. However, it also set the stage for both admiration and criticism, with some seeing him as decisive and others as brash and insensitive.

In hindsight, "The Apprentice" marked a pivotal point in Donald Trump's journey. It not only helped to reshape his public image but also primed him for a political career that few could have foreseen. The show's blend of entertainment and business showcased his ability to capture the public's attention and provided a glimpse into the traits that would later define his time in office as the 45th President of the United States.

For teenagers aspiring to venture into the entertainment industry, remember that success often stems from a combination of passion, perseverance, and continuous growth. The path may be challenging, but it's also incredibly rewarding. Embrace your uniqueness and use it as your strength, as the industry values authenticity.

Stay dedicated to honing your skills, whether it's acting, singing, dancing, or any other creative pursuit. Seek out opportunities for learning and improvement, whether through classes, workshops, or practice sessions. Don't be afraid to take risks and put yourself out there – auditions, open mics, and talent shows can be great stepping stones.

Surround yourself with a supportive network of friends, family, mentors, and peers who share your passion. They can provide valuable insights, feedback, and encouragement during both the highs and lows of your journey.

Remember, success rarely comes overnight. Stay patient and persistent, celebrating even the small victories along the way. Rejections and setbacks are part of the process, but they can also be valuable learning experiences that fuel your growth.

Lastly, keep your love for your craft alive. The entertainment industry can be demanding, so nurturing your passion will help you maintain your enthusiasm and drive over the long run. Stay true to yourself, work hard, and never stop believing in your dreams – your journey in the entertainment industry is yours to shape and conquer.

Chapter 6

Stepping into the World of Politics

Presidential Candidacy Announcement:

Hey friend, Buckle up, because we're diving into the moment when the world of politics met the world of reality TV and real estate. Imagine this: it's June 16, 2015, and you're scrolling through your social media feed. Suddenly, you see a headline that makes you rub your eyes in disbelief – "Donald Trump Announces He's Running for President!" Yep, you read it right, and it's not a prank. The man known for his skyscrapers, catchphrases, and firing people on TV just threw his hat into the political ring. Talk about a plot twist!

So why is this such a big deal? Well, picture this: you're watching "The Apprentice," a show where people compete for a job with Trump, and now he's saying he wants a job... as the President! It's like a real-life version of the shows you love, with a twist you never saw coming.

Now, let's break it down. Donald Trump was already a household name, thanks to his flashy buildings, business deals, and those two famous words – "You're Fired!" He'd spent years building a brand as a tough, no-nonsense business mogul on TV. And now, he's saying he wants to take that same

"You're Fired!" energy and apply it to the entire country. It's like a superhero deciding to switch from fighting villains to running a whole city – unexpected and intriguing.

But hold on, there's more! Trump's announcement was met with a mix of reactions. Some people thought, "Hey, he's a successful businessman, he knows how to get things done." Others were scratching their heads, wondering if this was just a publicity stunt. And let's not forget the skeptics who said, "Wait, can a reality TV star really be a leader?"

The thing is, whether you agreed with him or not, you couldn't ignore it. Trump's announcement shook up the political landscape. It was like a disruptor walking into a room where everyone was used to the same old speeches and politicians. Love him or not, he brought something different to the table, and that got people talking.

And you know what, friend? This moment isn't just history; it's a lesson in dreaming big and challenging expectations. Imagine if you decided to take a leap into something unexpected. Maybe you're into coding, art, or sports, and suddenly you decide to switch things up and do something no one saw coming. That's the spirit that Trump's announcement brought to the political stage – a reminder that sometimes, the best moves are the unexpected ones.

So, the next time you find yourself daydreaming about what you could achieve, remember that in 2015, a businessman turned reality TV star shocked the world by announcing he wanted to lead the country. It's a reminder that the most exciting stories often start with a twist that no one saw coming.

Key Campaign Promises:

During his presidential campaign, Donald Trump outlined several key promises that resonated with a significant portion of the American population. He pledged to prioritize job creation and economic growth by renegotiating trade deals and bringing back jobs to the U.S. His stance on immigration, particularly building a border wall and tightening immigration policies, generated both fervent support and opposition. Another central promise was to repeal and replace the Affordable Care Act, also known as Obamacare. These promises formed the core of his campaign message, capturing the attention of voters across the nation.

The 45th President of the United States:

Against the odds, Donald Trump secured an electoral victory in the 2016 presidential election, becoming the 45th President of the United States. His victory marked a historic moment, given his status as an outsider to the traditional political establishment. His inauguration in January 2017 was met with both celebration and protest, underscoring the deeply divided nature of the country.

Election Victory and Inauguration:

The inauguration marked the transition from campaign promises to tangible action. It was a moment when Trump's vision for the country began to take shape. Supporters hoped his unconventional approach and outsider perspective would bring about positive change, while critics were wary of the potential impact of his policies on various fronts.

Notable Policies and Initiatives:

During his time in office, Donald Trump implemented a range of policies that left a significant mark on the nation. His administration pursued tax reform, resulting in the Tax Cuts and Jobs Act of 2017, which aimed to stimulate economic growth. Trump also focused on deregulation, aiming to reduce government oversight and create a more business-friendly environment.

His administration made significant changes to immigration policies, with a particular emphasis on border security. The travel ban on citizens from certain countries, the "zero tolerance" policy on illegal border crossings, and efforts to curtail so-called sanctuary cities were all prominent aspects of his approach to immigration.

Foreign policy-wise, Trump's administration engaged in negotiations with North Korea and brokered diplomatic agreements between Israel and some Arab nations, known as the Abraham Accords. However, his foreign policy decisions, such as withdrawing from the Paris Agreement on climate change and the Iran nuclear deal, were met with both support and criticism.

These are just a few highlights of Donald Trump's time in office. It's important to approach these topics with a critical and open mindset, considering various perspectives and sources to form a well-rounded understanding of his presidency. Whether you view his time as President positively or negatively, studying his tenure can provide valuable insights into the complexities of leadership, politics, and the impact of policy decisions on a nation.

Whether you cheered or cringed during Trump's presidency, one thing's for sure – it was a chapter in American history that won't be forgotten. His unconventional approach, his Twitter diplomacy, his connection with some segments of the population – all of these left an indelible mark on the nation.

So, as you learn about this period, remember that understanding history means looking at the big picture. Dive into different sources, seek various perspectives, and form your own opinion. Whether you're talking about Trump's policies or the reactions they sparked, his time in office is a lesson in the power of leadership, the complexities of governance, and the lasting impact of decisions on a nation and its people.

Chapter 7

Lessons from Donald Trump

Resilience and Persistence:

Hey, future leaders! Let's dive into some key lessons we can learn from Donald Trump's journey. One of the biggest takeaways is resilience and persistence. Imagine this: a businessman and TV star faces countless challenges and obstacles, yet he keeps pushing forward. Whether you agree with his methods or not, there's something to be said about not giving up when things get tough.

Think about your own dreams and goals. There will be setbacks, doubts, and moments when it feels like the world is against you. But remember, just like Trump, you have the power to stand back up, learn from your mistakes, and keep moving forward. Resilience means bouncing back stronger after every fall, and persistence means never giving up, even when the odds are stacked against you.

Business and Entrepreneurial Insights:

Now, let's talk about business and entrepreneurship. Trump's journey from real estate to reality TV to the presidency is a masterclass in thinking outside the box and seizing opportunities. Imagine being a teen with a wild idea – maybe starting a small business, creating your own app, or even organizing events. Just like Trump, you can turn your passions and skills into something amazing.

Trump's business insights teach us that risk-taking and innovation can lead to success. He wasn't afraid to take calculated risks, and he knew the importance of branding and marketing. Think about how you can apply these principles to your own ventures. Whether you're into coding, art, writing, or any other field, embracing your unique skills and ideas can set you on a path to greatness.

Understanding Political Landscape:

Okay, let's shift gears and talk politics. Trump's journey from TV to the White House shows us that understanding the political landscape is crucial. Imagine this: stepping into the world of politics with no prior experience. It's like being dropped into a maze with hidden traps and secret doors. But guess what? Trump navigated it – for better or worse.

As teens, you might not be ready to run for office just yet, but understanding the basics of politics is essential. You live in a world where decisions made by leaders impact your life, so being informed is key. Take the time to learn about different viewpoints, policies, and the power of voting. Educate yourself, ask questions, and stay curious about how the political system works.

Remember, just like in any chapter of history, there are lessons to be learned from Trump's journey. Resilience and persistence, the courage to innovate in business, and the importance of understanding the political landscape – these are all tools you can use to shape your own future. The story of Donald Trump isn't just about him; it's a chance for you to reflect on your own dreams, aspirations, and the path you want to carve out in this world. So, go out there, be bold, and make your mark, future leaders!

The Conclusion

Congratulations, curious minds, on completing this journey through the life and journey of a prominent figure – Donald Trump. As you close the chapters of this book, take a moment to reflect on the lessons, insights, and inspiration you've gained from exploring the life of the 45th President of the United States.

Donald Trump's story is not just about politics; it's about the power of ambition, the courage to step into uncharted territories, and the determination to leave a lasting impact. Whether you view his journey positively or critically, there are valuable takeaways that can shape your own path.

From real estate mogul to reality TV star to President, Trump's journey is a testament to the power of ambition. It's a reminder that dreaming big and setting audacious goals can propel you forward, even when faced with obstacles. His story shows that success often requires perseverance and the willingness to overcome challenges that come your way.

Trump's business ventures and branding strategies offer insights into creative thinking and innovation. Just like him, you can leverage your unique talents and interests to create something remarkable. Whether it's a small project, a startup idea, or a creative pursuit, don't be afraid to think outside the box and explore new avenues.

Understanding the political world is not just reserved for politicians. Trump's journey from businessman to President underscores the importance of being informed about the decisions that impact our society. Even if you're not planning a career in politics, being aware of the political landscape empowers you to engage with the world around you and advocate for the changes you believe in.

Controversy often surrounds prominent figures, and Donald Trump is no exception. His presidency sparked intense debates, discussions, and reflections on the direction of the country. Just as his actions prompted diverse reactions, your choices and decisions will shape your impact on the world.

Embrace the opportunity to challenge norms, question the status quo, and contribute to meaningful change.

As you put down this book, remember that you have the power to shape your own journey. Your dreams, ambitions, and passions are uniquely yours. Whether you're interested in business, entertainment, politics, or any other field, the lessons from Donald Trump's journey are applicable to your own path.

Embrace the resilience, innovation, and determination that marked Trump's journey. Learn from his successes and failures, and let them guide you as you carve out your own story. Just as he faced adversity, navigated uncharted territories, and left an impact on the world, you too have the potential to create a story that leaves a mark on history.

So, future leaders, keep dreaming big, keep pushing boundaries, and keep learning from the journeys of those who came before you. The world is waiting for your ideas, your innovations, and your contributions. As you reflect on the life and journey of Donald Trump, let it be a source of inspiration as you step boldly into the exciting chapters of your own life.

Made in the USA
Monee, IL
27 November 2024